Liquid Rainbows

Crosslake, Minnesota
Then and Now

VICKI MICKELSON

the PeppertreePress, LLC
Sarasota, Florida

Copyright © Vicki Mickelson, 2021

All rights reserved. Published by the Peppertree Press, LLC.
The Peppertree Press and associated logos are trademarks of
the Peppertree Press, LLC.

No part of this publication may be reproduced, stored in a retrieval
system, transmitted in any form or by any means, electronic,
mechanical, photocopying, recording, or otherwise, without prior
written permission of the publisher and author/illustrator.
Graphic design by Rebecca Barbier.

For information regarding permission,
call 941-922-2662 or contact us at our website:
www.peppertreepublishing.com or write to:
the Peppertree Press, LLC.
Attention: Publisher
1269 First Street, Suite 7
Sarasota, Florida 34236

ISBN: 978-1-61493-773-9

Library of Congress Number: 2021909020

Printed May 2021

Dedication:

For
Larry, Susan, Cindy, Shari, Craig and Becky,
my cabin crew

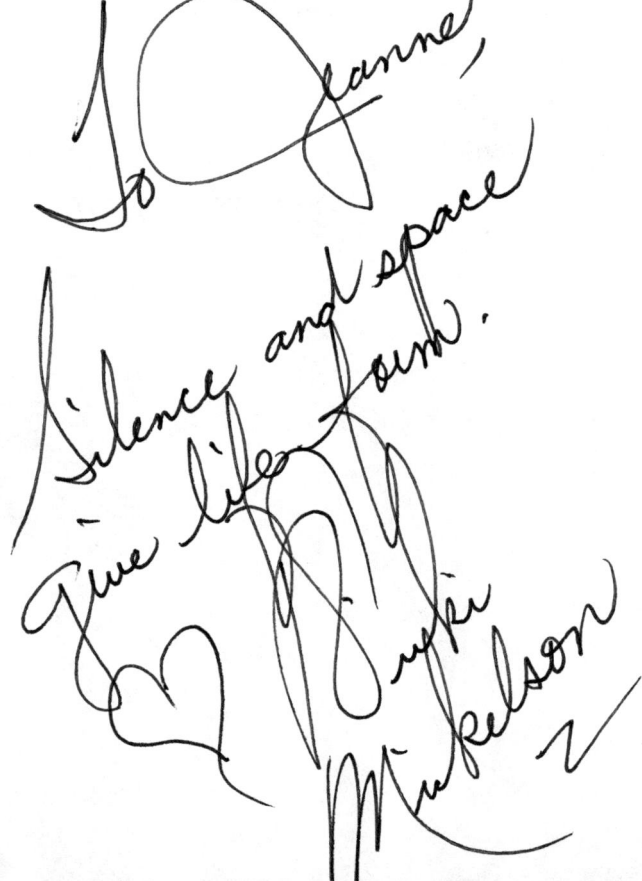

To Jeanne,
Silence and space
give life room.

Lyn Mikelson

Vicki Mickelson is also the author of:

Under the Crumbling Stars

Dearest Liberty

Island Attitudes

Blades to Ballet Shoes

Island Interludes

Frozen Symmetry

Shamrock Savvy

Island Melodies

Acknowledgements

Thank you to my cousins and brother for providing me with fun attitudes, exuberant energy and listening ears during our summer vacation cabin adventures.

To my island writing rats, hugs for your distance learning sessions. I treasure your feedback.

Julie Ann and Teri Lynn of Peppertree Press, as always, your support is greatly appreciated.

Debbie and Bill, my gratitude for trusting me with your yellow sea cottage, which is such a source of inspiration.

An abundance of thanks to my readers. Your positive comments and unfaltering love for my poetry keep the pen in my hand.

Table of Contents

The Happiest of Landings 1	We "C" You 38
Outhouse Blues 4	Over the Top 40
Muddled Masses 6	Wrap It Up! 42
Landing Happily 8	The Bung 44
Purple Peanut 10	Ready With Reed's 46
Bouffant Bedazzled 13	Give it Up for the Gallery 48
Echoez of Echo Ridge 15	Not Hard to Ware 50
Daggett Lake Rescue 17	The Perks of Pine Peaks 52
Trolling for Doughnuts 19	Let's Go Italian 54
Couldn't be More Ideal 21	The Cedar Chest 56
Daggett Dreams Deferred 23	Norway Nuances 58
Manhattan's For All 25	Wharf Whimsy 60
Blazing Blazer 27	Lundrigan's Lost 62
Honeymoon Haven 30	Celebrate! Celebrate! 64
May I Exchange? 32	Loon Love 66
Moonlite Bay 34	Liquid Rainbows 69
Andy's Reimagined 36	

The Happiest of Landings

Happy Landing was my week-long vacation haven
An avalanche of excitement
Ignited in me each July
As I packed for our family trip
And the three hours driving north
Seemed like an eternity
As we lurched forward
The harsh reality of leaving friends
Was not an issue
My cousins would be my cohorts and confidantes
We were summer pioneers
A not-so-paranoid species of fools
Flitting to unearth fungi of any kind
On Cross Lake
Of the Whitefish Chain

Each family had a stark cabin
With flickering light bulbs
Hanging from the ceilings
Moth-eaten, hand-stitched bedroom quilts
An antique gas stove
And an unfashionable outhouse many yards away

My dad brought his 2 1/2 HP Johnson motor
For the rowboat provided for each cabin
My brother brought his tattered stuffed dog
My mom brought added kitchen tools – pans, spatulas
I brought my fantasies

We slept in
Sluggishly slipping into bathing suits
And heading to the lake
Where the dock was our tanning bed
Inner tubes our afternoon floating devices
On which we concocted
Gymnastic moves worthy of Olympic medals
From which we caught minnows with our hands
To use as bait on rowboat fishing excursions
Building up our muscles with oars
And in the reeds of warm water
We'd sling out our cane poles
In hopes of catching a perch or pumpkin-bellied sunny

When the minnows and worms were depleted
We reached inside a Mr. Salty Pretzel box
Yanked out brown sticks
Soaked them in lake water
Eased them on our hooks
Hurled them out and hoisted up pan fish beauties
For our dinner

Our moms fried them up in cast iron pans
Smothered with butter
And for dessert
We ate pie made from wild blueberries
We had picked from bushes nearby

At night we reflected on our day
Chatting late after numerous games of cards
Washed out our bathing suits
Hung them outside on the line to dry
And realized
We had made
The happiest of landings

Outhouse Blues

Each summer in Minnesota
Was highlighted
By a week-long lake vacation
With my paternal cousins
We looked forward to swimming
Sharing log cabins with our families
Fishing from rowboats
Equipped with my dad's 2½ HP Johnson
And Mr. Salty pretzels for bait
Picking blueberries for homemade pies
The crusts dotted with granulated sugar
Sunning on the dock
On top of worn terry beach towels
At Happy Landing Resort
On Cross Lake

Our one gripe
Was trudging to outhouses
To relieve ourselves
Among a collage of pine trees
Under a rinse of morning light
Or in the shadow
Of a midnight flashlight

After hoisting our butts
And hunkering down on wooden cutout circles
In a frenzy of urgency
We worried a black bear
Upon smelling the fragrant aroma
Would caress the mini structure
And howl the blues
Under scudding clouds
Leaving us trapped
To sing the blues
As well

Muddled Masses

The glass case
In the office of Happy Landing Resort
Was home
To a wide array of candy bars
To fussily explore

We cousins always had nickels
In our pockets
In case we decided to take a detour
From our do-nothing days
And clamp our eyes on the beauties
Like seals on the edge of a glacier

The curled wrappers
Some crinkled
Some with slightly melted insides
Signaled to their parallel parts
We were there
Undecided
With jingling coins
Having a soiree
Probing their way to cotton depths
Waiting for us to purge them
For
Baby Ruths, Snickers and Almond Joys
From their solitary confinement

To declare glass case winners
In the chocolate pageant

We always positioned our elbows
On top of the antique counter
Like scavengers
And
Made our wavering decisions

I usually chose a Heath Bar
With almond-spattered toffee
Drowning in milk chocolate
A small bar compared to others
But I would snatch my prize
Crowning her the queen
In the muddled mess
Of dripping brown
Quenching my cocoa hunger
And leaving my pocket devoid of nickels

Landing Happily

At Happy Landing Resort
The atmosphere was always aflutter
Like Mr. Rogers' Neighborhood
Predictable but varied

The sun streaked its way
Over the surrendering side hills in the early mornings
Blazing its path
To align with the fickle water
Creating a glimmering tremor
In its depth
Like an inside tornado
Beckoning us cousins
To lazily harness our energy
Get a no-sunscreen tan
Wade into the sandy-bottomed Cross Lake
Float on black tire inner tubes
The harsh, hot rubber
A buffer for the nipping minnows and perch
Flittering beneath our sagging butts
Or
Jump into a wooden rowboat
Brandish cane fishing poles
And
A supply of pretzels
To use for bait
Row to the reedy weeds

In a shallow tattering of sun-speckled bay
To fish for pumpkin-bellied sunnies
That our dads would scale, sever heads and gut
And our moms would fry
In cast iron pans slathered in butter
For dinner

Crunching the egg-washed, flour-dipped curled whoppers
The faceless filets
Were pivotal
In our fishing trial
And
Shattered any expectations
Of not
Landing happily

Purple Peanut

The town of Pine River
About half an hour from Crosslake
Back in the 60's
Was home to the hottest teen dance club
The Purple Peanut
Famous for its Minnesota-bred live bands
The grimy, purple-painted building
Rocked with the beat of ear-shattering music
And a horde of teen girls
Dancing and hovering around the cute guys
Pounding their drums
Strumming bass guitars
And bellowing lead vocals
Shaking strands of greasy hair from their faces

My cousins and I lived for the Peanut
It was a must destination during our cabin vacations
Even if we had to put up with my brother & younger cousin
Who roamed the perimeter, pacing
Sometimes creating a menace
Out of boredom

That didn't stop us girls from flirting with band members
Whose skinny hips
Barely held up black jeans
And whose trash was left as debris
At the end of the show

Over the years
I fumbled away from the Peanut
With two loves
One was a round-faced curly-haired blond
Decked out in denim overalls
We were immediately drawn to each other
Clasped hands, danced and never left each other's side
My braces were not a barrier
To a brush of lips
So subtle
So mind shattering

We parted with tear-filled eyes
When our parents pulled up in their cars
And the liquid spilled over
Down his cheeks and mine
I never learned his name

Mike, the drummer of The Predators
Was my other love
His band played the Peanut
And his smile haunted me
As his drumsticks slammed to the sky

During a break
We chatted, exchanged addresses
Shimmied against each other
And pondered our future
The relationship, mostly long distance
Lasted two years

His band occasionally played in Minneapolis
And I would attend
We wrestled with a desire to be
More than pen pals
But that was a foggy mirage
And clarity kicked in
After he spent a year in college
In a psychedelic haze
Then
Sent me a silver peanut charm
For my turquoise inlaid bracelet
With a note
"We'll always have the Purple Peanut"

Bouffant Bedazzled

In our teens
My cousins and I
Spent our cabin days in a blur
Of sun tanning
On the elongated dock
Or
Jetting out
In the tepid Cross Lake water
In paint-chipped wooden rowboats
Rocking on mini waves
That caressed the sun sparkles
Glinting in our eyes
As we stared
Reeling in the posh beauty

Rested and eager
We were always ready for evening action
So one night we secured a car
For a nighttime romp

The echo of summer our impetus
We cruised to the Dairy Queen
The only hot spot in town
Without a dimming spirit

Bouffant
Mellow and predatory

Entered our lives
In a bangled swoosh
Hair teased and sprayed
He pursued in a frenzy
And got our attention
His essence created enduring sparks

Snippets of snickered comments
Permeated our conversations
But he especially was on the prowl
For Cindy

So when he showed up
The following day
At the resort
Bouffant was unprepared
To be faced with Uncle Cliff's FBI shoulder holster
Discreetly hidden beneath a blazer
Holding a polished gun
That bedazzled
Sparking fireworks in Bouffant's saucer eyes
When revealed
Prompting him to immediately turn
Without a word
Scamper away quickly
With raised eyebrows
And
Hair reaching toward the sun

Echoez of Echo Ridge

The half-moon driveway
Overlooking Cross Lake on Route 66
Flows in a fantasy fashion
Like the backdrop of a movie
Creating a majestic solitude
Sacrificing itself to crunchy pinecones
Beneath the tall spindly trees of wilderness
Trampled by my cousins, aunts, uncles, parents, brother and me
As we infiltrated Echo Ridge Supper Club
Ravenous in a vision of eternal glory
Infatuated by the labyrinth of royal beauty

Inside the hill-hanging structure
Background notes emanated in bubbly tones
Like Lawrence Welk's champagne music

We annually dressed up one night of our vacation week
For the fancy experience
Of linen napkins, crystal goblets
Mini vases with wild flowers
Baskets heaping with rolls
And packets of real butter
The appetizer tray perked us up
With its pimento cheese stuffed celery
Pickles, sliced tomatoes and peppers

The flavors floated across our tongues like a conveyor
There was no way to stave them off
I always grappled with the menu
Usually settled on the fried shrimp
Sometimes, if we were extra fortunate
A scoop of peppermint ice cream
Would be the finishing touch
To the meal
And we would barely be able to rise
From the table
Inwardly pleading to be rescued

And now
The half-moon driveway
On the shore of Cross Lake
Still exists
At least in essence
Right next to Zorbaz
Where I still grapple with an extensive menu
But there are no linen napkins
No fresh flowers on the tables
Customers order at the bar
Picnic tables are scattered on the back deck
With a view of the sand volleyball pit
And boaters dock and climb
To order pizza, zpaghetti and taco saladz
Listen to the throbbing music
And the echoez
Of Echo Ridge

Daggett Lake Rescue

On an ordinary day
My cousins and I met a couple of guys in Crosslake
We found out through flirty conversation
Their cabin was on Daggett Lake
An adjoining lake to ours
We knew our parents wouldn't be thrilled
In fact, the boys would probably be taboo
But we tingled with anticipation
At seeing them again
So we concocted a distorted teenage plan
Lunging forward with it
Whispering about our scheme for the following day
Hoping we wouldn't collapse in gripping tears
If they found out

The next day
I pleaded with my dad to let me take the boat and motor
Even though I was smeared with guilt
I teased him with revelations
That we wouldn't be gone long

Minutes later we squinted against the dancing sun
Revved up the Johnson
Our hair and makeup perfect
And skimmed the mini waves
Ready to devour our gorgeous hunks

We squiggled on bench seats and headed across the lake
Through the channel
Past C&C Boat Works
In no wake mode
Using our hands as shields
To keep our hair intact
Clinching our appeal as hot chicks

We entered Daggett Lake
And began to scout our hotties
Dangling our enigmatic actions
In front of the Fabio brothers' cabin
We spiraled our listless boat
Around and around
With intent to run out of gas
As we orbited the lake
Our hearts throbbing with hope

Just as I was certain my navigation was futile
The Johnson sputtered and sputtered and spurt
And our skin goose bumped as our beautiful, brazen boys
Rescued us
In their flashy red streamlined speed boat
Laughing hilariously

Trolling for Doughnuts

The little rowboat with the 2 1/2 HP Johnson
Never sat still
At the Happy Landing dock
Except after sunset smeared the sky
And the lake became a portrait of color
Even early in the mornings
When the horizon was a halo of gritty solace
Creating a dust of swirled glow
My mom and aunts hurled themselves
Out of lumpy beds
Maneuvered into cotton shorts and sleeveless blouses
Squinted at the sky's duet of hues
Sprayed a sea of Aqua Net on their cratered curls
Plopped in the mini cruiser
Revved up the engine
That pulsated in tune to the lake's ripples
Zigzagged across the glinting clacking
Of trembling early-morning water
Slammed up on the downtown shore
Where they yanked the boat up on the sand
Then trudged up the hill to the bakery
Never wavering in their gait
Their mouths yacking away
Their arms jerking in gesture
Their eyes wincing at the July sun guzzling their skin

The busiest place in the morning
Sold sugary revelations
The trio lingered
Hunched over glass cases
And
Snatched two dozen sculpted beauties

Cinnamon rolls drizzled with white frosting
Glazed apple fritters gooey with grease
Bismarcks stuffed with raspberry jam
Lemon filled pastries
Maple frosted long johns
And cake doughnuts with sprinkles
Because
That's why they got up early
Jumped in a rowboat
Forged their way to the bakery
To troll
For doughnuts
For breakfast

Couldn't be More Ideal

On the way to Norway Ridge Supper Club
Down quivering, winding County Road 16
Is Ideal Township
A thoroughly quaint town
Without much more than the Milwaukee Club
A dive bar and restaurant easily passed by
And a fire department
Which was the exotic building of interest
For my cousins and me
Primitive in structure, yes
Abstract in our minds, of course
A stoic low brick rectangle, slightly slanted
Propped in a mini forest of Up North pine trees
Never wavered in its multi-use
Surrendering to trampling teens
On Saturday nights
Where small town and city kids collided
Thrashing to bass beats
Rummaging the crowd to find dance partners
Then merging
They scooted between thorny throngs
Listening to whacked-out groovy sounds
That came in waves

We were enamored with the lyrical ambiance
The multitude of sweaty bodies dissolved and pinched
Shifting in a blurred yowling of voices
Eventually chiming for us

After convincing our hesitant parents to drop us off
Like lost pebbles on a gravel driveway
We stabbed the stagnant arc of movement
Shedding the myth of controversy
Seeped into the arid air
Splayed ourselves across the dance floor
Clutched each other loosely in crinkled concoctions
And entangled ourselves
In the atmosphere of the fire hall
Which couldn't have been
More Ideal

Daggett Dreams Deferred

Daggett Brook was originally an upscale store
Showcasing artwork, pottery
Some hokey trinkets
That weekly cabin renters desired
Such as shot glasses and back scratchers
Embellished with "Crosslake"
And a glorious array of women's fashions
Classic patterns and styles
That changed seasonally
Unique brands not found elsewhere
It was rumored several Minneapolis teachers
Lurked in the racks' shadows every summer
Flinging year-long wardrobes on the counter
To purchase
In muffled glee

Then came the store's makeover
No more local artwork
Or stunning pottery that transformed a room
Prickling one's senses
To hover in vicious probing for meaning
The trinkets crumbled in a disappearing act
But the thirst was quenched
With bold fashion
Tangible evidence there was a rebirth

And clientele clamored to scoop up
The Minnetonka moccasins
Shimmery jeweled special occasion frocks
And a slew of Crosslake gear
Bounding from hangers and folded on tables
Along with charismatic cabin wear
And delicately painted wooden boxes
To hold gems and treasures
Of
Deferred Daggett Brook
Dreams

Manhattan's For All

As teens
My brother and I cruised our speedboat
Zipping around the Whitefish Chain of 14 lakes
In northern Minnesota
We catapulted the craft
With an open throttle
Bounding from Cross Lake
To Rush to Lower Whitefish
To Trout Lake
Where the water shimmered in sea green
Flinging our scantily-clad bodies
In relentless spasms
To his on-tune solos
And my toxic-tone dead drawls
Of the Beetles and Herman's Hermits
Creating our own chaos
In the bow of the boat
Wired on the muttering of the motor
And dulled by the wail of
No wake sputterings
Meandering through the many narrow channels
Still dizzy as we slantily gazed
At our lake crowd
Clattering in vicious competition
For the honor of pummeling onto the sand shore
To ponder the listless afternoon

We hoisted and anchored
Out of the sapphire blue water
In chants of orchestral trickles
Stranded in head fog
Never flinching
Just looking cool in tattered tedium
Lazily sipping sodas
And embraced
The shore of Manhattan Beach
Staking our territory

Manhattan's now has boat boys
Who park one's boat
For tips
And one can no longer lazily linger
On the shore
With just a bloody Mary in hand
One must
Wait for a table
And order a meal

Inclusive?
Or
Exclusive?

Blazing Blazer

Twenty minutes south of Crosslake
Is the enchanting resort town of Nisswa
Dotted with treasured boutiques
A candy store
Several restaurants
One of them an old-fashioned A&W drive-in
Where root beer floats
And Papa burgers
Are devoured
A hardware store full of souvenirs and necessities
A well-equipped sporting goods dealer
And in the 60's
The Blazer
The infamous teen dance venue
Rumbling with live bands
Like the Del Counts
A legend from the Twin Cities
With a posse of groupies

The epic guitars and drums
Were the glue
Of the arcade that inhabited the building
Fibrous souls
Fragile in their sulkiness
Grazed the mashed humid interior

Adequately accepting Oscars in their minds
For their bumbling and ruthless attempts
To score
With a verbal blip
Or tattered lapping of lips
And I was one of them
Clutching at the hem of my hot pants
Easing them over my tanned thighs
To cover my behind
Then with arched arms forming canyons
Cheering on the band
Immune to spit bubbles splattered on my neck hair
Like mosquitoes on a windshield

One night
From behind
A hand grabs mine
Leads me through the hulking horde
Outside
Where we shyly giggle
Explain we are shocked each other is there
Up North
At The Blazer
We two friends
Who have known each other since we were five
Who were square dance partners
In elementary school gym class
Who spent most of the senior all night party together bowling

Who now
Are locking lips passionately
Thrust up against a 1958 DeSoto
Saliva dripping down my chin
Instead of the back of my neck
And
In the background
The Blazer blazing

Honeymoon Haven

We were married in August of 1972
Outdoors
On a wild game farm
I wore a white eyelet peasant dress
With a purple underskirt
And lace-up cumber bun
White leather ballet shoes adorned my feet
Blond hair cascaded down my back
My head was bare
My bouquet was a mixture of purple flowers
Plucked from neighbors' gardens that morning
Jerry was dapper in white polyester bell bottoms
An embroidered multi-colored belt
A purple and white crepe shirt
White tie
Ponytail
"Color my World" by Chicago filled the grounds
We recited our own vows
In front of 200 friends and family

Our honeymoon at Manhattan Beach
Was to be short and romantic
Little money and Mom's upcoming surgery
Were deciding factors

But when we arrived
Still flinching in revel

Of our hippie wedding
With a turkey and wild rice buffet
Cold Duck flowing from a fountain
My brother's band playing "Whiter Shade of Pale"
As the processional
We found
The lodge sodden with rain
Flooded
Leaving us stranded
In a flux of disbelief

We were stymied as to where we would linger
For three days
Until the manager made a call
And
Secured us a cabin elsewhere
Offered us a white linen dinner
Making sure the transition was not jumbled

We scanned the sky
Awash with stripes of pink and lavender
Smeared in beautiful patterns
Beckoning us
To our honeymoon haven
Across the channel from the Wharf
Where we set up our Hibachi grill
Snuggled in flannel shirts
Watched boats whisper by
Never missing the
Manhattan Magic

May I Exchange?

On our very brief honeymoon in 1972
We were ready to rock
And what better place to dress up
Dance to a live band
Have a cocktail and groove
Than The Exchange in downtown Crosslake
With an overflowing young clientele
In disco gear
A subdued lighting concept
Hiding spilled beer
It was the hot spot

There were swaddled seniors looming
Dangling their dripping Tom Collinses
From arthritic fingers
Their crinkled flesh cinched into tight waistbands
Smug in their shattered youth
Blinking back smoke tears
With shaggy hair absorbing the tainted air
As the fuchsia sky bloomed after sunset

I remember my red and white print maxi halter dress
The white crocheted shawl
Draped around my shoulders
The red patent mini-heeled sandals
That were easy to dance in

After the parking lot filled up
It was like combat inside
Space was at a premium
But we were lucky to grab a bench-seat booth
Elated as gulls
With
Wings flapping furiously
Full of love
Full of energy
Full of anticipation
We were acrobats on the dance floor
Jerry's shuffling platform shoes
Coincided with others' karate moves
We were a spectacle under shallow light
Clinching our future in shadows

And now
After a fire
The Exchange is no longer
The parking lot is missing stumbling young adults
And
Seniors rushing to get home
For the 10:00 news

Cars with For Sale signs litter the lot
Boats and RV's wait for new owners

The energy is gone
The music has dissipated
May I make an exchange?

Moonlite Bay

Huddled in a majestic corner
Of radiant Cross Lake
Where Route 66 meets County Road 16
Sits the iconic Moonlite Bay Family Restaurant
Hovering on a hillside
Above a bay with the same name
Copious boat docks line the water
Steep stairs welcome patrons
The humongous deck
Supports picnic and high circular tables
Along with a gazebo bar
And numerous barstools facing the bay
Overlooking top-of-the-line
Premier pontoon boats

Beyond the deck
The log structure
Houses a casual Up North ambiance
Even a small dance floor
Where live bands used to play
And now is home to late night weekend DJ's
Most of the menu is average fare
The pizza, however
Is thin, crispy and seeping with flavor

The current restaurant
Is a pathetic contrast to the old supper club

That had tables draped in white linen
Animated waiters and waitresses formally dressed
In starched black and white uniforms
There as static figures in the theatrical feast

One evening during the week
On our annual Crosslake vacation
My family, aunts, uncles, and cousins
Dressed up to become actors
Immersed in a rehearsal
Stoically perusing the menu
Ordering succulent fried shrimp
Or crusty fried chicken
Or medium-rare sirloin steak
Or thin-boned frog legs
With baked potatoes and sour cream
And baskets of dinner rolls
Accompanied by pats of cold Land O'Lakes butter

Feverishly we devoured every scrap
Learning our lines
Blocking our moves
Becoming nearly invisible
In the Back-to-the-60's cartoonish spectacle
Botching our entrances and exits
And launching careers
In the
Bay of Moonlite experience

Andy's Reimagined

A classmate's grandparents
Owned a trailer near Crosslake
I envied him
Because that's where he spent his summers
And when he turned 15
He worked at Andy's Grocery
Earning money for his adventures
During the school year

My vision was to saturate my summers
With Up North
It was embedded in my mind
But never came to fruition
I had no permanent cabin
Perched on the Whitefish Chain
Even though my personal dreams persisted
I relented to spending
Just a week's vacation in the town
Stopping in to greet my friend
And continued to pierce my ambitions
With fantasy scenarios

Andy's continues to announce its existence
In bold letters
On the corner of Highway 3 and Route 66
But the town has evolved
And so has Andy's

Now
Andy's is a gray paint-splashed liquor store
Majorly musty with lumpy floors
A drippy humidor with cheap cigars
And high prices
The bleached blond cashier
Calls everyone 'honey'
And points next door to the adjoining restaurant
For lunch or dinner

Andy's Restaurant is somewhat worthy
The functionally landscaped outdoor area
Gets rave reviews
Pavers, bar, fire pit, umbrella tables
And pine tree views
But the mediocre food sits in one's stomach
In a grease pool

Andy's has transformed
It's still Andy's
No longer a grocery store
But reimagined
Anchored in a blur of booze
And a twirl of wind-twisted fire

We "C" You

On the channel between Cross Lake and Daggett
Is C&C Boat Works
An iconic mirror of what the town encompasses
A geometric building
Transformed over the years
It pulsates as the epicenter of business

If one wants to purchase a lobbed out pontoon
Where does one go?
If one needs a speedy ski boat
Where does one go?
If one needs a jet ski or paddle board
Where does one go?
How about a Big Mable float for tubing
Or a splash pad?
A sound system replacement
Sumptuous cushions
Wake boards
Life preservers, towropes
A nut, a bolt, a can cooler
A wet suit
Shrink-wrapped boat storage
Detailing, refurbishing
Motor upgrades, ladders, canvas covers
Repairs
Brad will fix you up
With all your needs

Igniting a long-lasting friendship
Altering anyone's perception that
Small town hospitality doesn't still exist

So even today
After many years in business
As boaters scan the landscape
A flicker of recognition emanates
Almost intuitively
And old customers turn right out of Cross Lake
In the solemn no wake zone
Slamming their motor into low
No longer shivering in the wind gusts
Awestruck at the silver sun
Not tainted by the menagerie
Of inflated floats strewn on the hill
Pull up to gas their boats
With motors gurgling
Passengers twitching
And silently utter
"We 'C' you"

Over the Top

One of my first stops when I came into town
Was Susan's Top Drawer
My favorite boutique on Route 66
Visits were always like winning the lottery
Bags of whimsical outfits made it
To the back of my car
Nestled between a cooler and sacks of groceries
They were my secret domain of stash

Susan's shop was slightly musty
With old carpet curled at the edges
That humped in humidity
Not a pleasant image
But I inhaled without thought
Knowing the treasures that existed within
Sometimes slanting awkwardly on their hangers
Or hanging on the walls like a trellis
Knew my zooming eyes would glance
And my arms would scoop them up
As Susan scooted closer to me
"Oh, oh, I have gorgeous specials for you"
That I brought back from my Punta Gorda store
Look at this – 50% off"
She'd flash her smeared smile
Retrieve blazers and jeans and capris
"Everything here you will love"
And of course she was right

I trembled as I accessorized from the jewelry counter
My prize one time was a snow cone bright
Cherry and grape chunky beaded necklace
That strangled my neck
Nearly leaving me weeping with awe

I made my exodus numerous times
From Susan's Top Drawer
Draped in new outfits and jewels
That I didn't need but couldn't resist

It was more than a boutique
It was a legacy
Whose snow cone bright pink and purple necklace beads
Live on in restrung neck attire
Created and worn by my granddaughter

And now
There is a thrift store occupying the space
A concession
That maybe houses some of those
Whimsical outfits
That were
Over the top

Wrap It Up!

There is only one gift shop in Crosslake
That is massive and all encompassing
A shop not tainted
Judy's House of Gifts
A huge log house
Etched in oozing Up North decor
Turned into a mecca of inventory
It juts out as a welcome
Art spurs reaction
That's what Judy's accomplishes

And she gift wraps
For any occasion

Thematic arrangements are awash inside
Holiday decor, seasonal accents, picture frames, kitchenware
All emerge unraveled
After the screen door slams
And one begins to imagine
The angel on your mantel
The placemats on your dining table
The leaping fish on your cabin wall
The Yankee candle's pine scent
Filtering through your family room
The floppy teddy bear's arms wrapped around your grandson
The mellow chime singing on your friend's deck

Judy's is a cavernous mix of perfect gifts
The ultimate shopping experience
Where you grab your item and smile
Set it on the counter
And say
"Wrap it up, please!"

The Bung

Emily has fewer than 1,000 people
It's a sleepy town on most days
But during the summer months
Cars scoot down Highway 6 through the town's center

For numerous years
Until a kitchen fire brought it to ruins
The Bungalow was a major dining destination
Entrancing patrons
It was a flashback to those fading restaurants
With an old Up North feel
Wobbly log tables and chairs
With deep nicks
Worn plastic cushioned booths
And paper placemats printed with a menu from the 1950's
The nuance remained in the log siding
The stone fireplace gnawed into the wall
Stuffed deer heads
Unraveled carpet
Acoustic clatter
And bar chatter blending in
From the adjoining dark abyss

I usually ordered the rib basket
With ribs smoked on the premises
Smothered in homemade BBQ sauce
Accompanied by a mound of fries
And a paper cup of slaw
Hovering on the side
That propelled my taste buds into far-flung oblivion
And even though the meal was upper crust
Accented with a red plastic water glass
It still remains
The small town dive
With a fly on the window
We refer to
As
The Bung

Ready With Reed's

Reed's is no longer a grimy little grocery
Across from Judy's House of Gifts
The once eerie entity without much content
Expanded into a slick array of all one needs
For a weekend or a week at the cabin

I have always looked forward
To my shopping stops
Grabbing a sturdy cart that stalwartly stands
Next to cute kiddie carts
Each with a protruding red flag
Perfect for the little ones to twinkle toe
Next to Mom or Dad, Grandma or Grandpa
And plunk a box of Cheerios,
Organic mac'n cheese, a squirt gun
Or bag of apples into their own cart

There is no melancholy in the store
Everyone is on a mission to stock up
Or grab and go
So the serene atmosphere is timeless
There are no raggedy edges like many
Small town grocery stores
Where dust covers the tops of cans
And the bakery goods
Are two days old

It's a breeze to maneuver past Ready-to-Eat
Fried chicken, mashed potatoes, corn and garlic toast
Past the gourmet cheese counter
Where I grab caraway Havarti
Several hunks
Past the deli where hard salami and tuna pasta salad
Are on my list
Then on to bakery goods
Wild rice bread is a must
I whip through produce
Selecting a cadre of organics
Gear toward the meat section
Tossing in Reed's homemade jerky and beef sticks
Grab paper towels and toilet paper
Then round to the final peripheral
Frozen Foods
Where I rarely shop at home
But Up North my taste buds mutate
Surging with flavor anticipation
So in a foggy haze
I guiltily lower a pint of Ben and Jerry's Cherry Garcia
Into my menagerie

And once again
Reed's was at the ready

Give it Up for the Gallery

Town Square has a plethora of business fronts
Some occasionally changing or vacant
But Lakes Area Gallery and Frame Shoppe
After moving from Highway 3
Has remained unsmudged
It is still bulging with a medley of gifts
Every item carefully selected
To celebrate Up North culture
Feisty cabin furnishings
In sync with those who love unique objects
It is an eclectic mix of local artists and more
Who create artwork
That squeezes out metaphor and comic intent

Like a gumshoe investigator
Peeling back the neutrality and relishing in ecstasy
It is easy to slither through the small shop
Grabbing a children's book
Or a Life is Good T-shirt
Stroll through the handmade jewelry counter
Past a wall of hand-dipped candles
Strut through a display of floor lamps
And collapse on an Adirondack chair
Made from water skis

But the big draw
Is in the back room
Where artistic framing skills are exhibited
Where Kristi and Pete and their well-trained staff
Do their thing for patrons
Who sometimes drive many many miles
To hail

Give it up for the Gallery

Not Hard to Ware

What is a small town without a hardware store
It's a staple, a necessity
Like ducks on a pond
Because we all chisel our way through projects
Needing drills, sandpaper, screwdrivers
We act like apprentices
Equipped with pouches
Filled with nails, hammers, and levels
We pound and measure and eyeball our efforts
Evolving into trade masters
And we tingle at the science fiction movie
Playing in our minds

Ace Hardware in Crosslake, MN
Is more than a go-to for screws and nuts
It's a destination that entices
Especially in the summer
When Adirondack chairs are perched on the roof
In coral, lime green, yellow, ruddy red and cobalt
And stacked in front
Twenty chairs high
Often lopsided

We sometimes enter just to browse
At the espresso machines, paint colors, fishing gear
The flip-flops, hummingbird feeders, grills
And my favorites — Lodge cast iron pans

If you need wine glasses — no problem
A stove, refrigerator, dishwasher — no problem
A life vest, a rain jacket — no problem
Birdseed, candy bars, towel racks, toilet seats — no problem
Beach toys, noodles, fishing poles
Outdoor furniture, wind chimes, rain gauges
Keys duplicated, a ball cap
Greeting cards, beach towels
Shower curtain, soap dish, soap, toilet bowl cleaner
Or underwear — no problem
Because Ace
Is not hard to ware

The Perks of Pine Peaks

As I was decorating for Christmas
I realized my favorite decoration
Was not a red glittered reindeer
Or the Swedish tomtes that mingle on a shelf
Or a red sequin satin pillow on the couch
Or the sparkly gold trio of trees and glittery star
On the glass coffee table
That glint when the Christmas tree lights twinkle
And force me to exhale in seasonal awe
It's the crunchy lime green malleable mesh fabric
That I drape in cascades
From ledges in the dining area
Like plumes of peacock feathers
That waft when I pass by

It was purchased on a thick cardboard roll
At Pine Peaks Gift Shop
That is attached to the Pine Peaks Restaurant
And also in the zone
A few feet away is the Pine Peaks Motel

I'm always dazed with a blast of stylish décor
When I enter the shop
Whether it's earthy flower arrangements
Christmas trees hung with silvery angels

Petrified wood sculptures
Books about loons
Napkins imprinted with pinecones
Or
Wreaths and silk flowers

Upstairs I've snatched baby outfits
Flower printed umbrellas
Toys for the grandchildren

I feel anything but shallow
Each time I experience
The swirl of intrigue
It's never a charade
Because
I know I am lucky
To have
The perk of Pine Peaks

Let's Go Italian

When I ventured Up North to the cabin
I refused to worry about dinner
So often
As I reached the town of Deerwood
With the leaping deer statue
I dialed up Mauciari's
Ordered spaghetti with meatballs
Italian salad and garlic bread
My go-to meal to gush over
However, I realized devouring the saucy dish
With homemade gravy from a family recipe
Blasted my weight up about
Ten pounds a summer
So I switched to a large supreme pizza
Delectable hand tossed crispy crust
Fresh green pepper, pepperoni and home-crafted sausage
Tasty, trance-like goodness
A positive vibe to ingest
From a funky restaurant
That refrains from the sullen
Possessing an Italian aura – homey and welcoming
It gurgles with testy bar conversation
And the warm scuttle of a family tratoria

Now I stop on my way to the cabin
Peek into the kitchen
Crouch on a bar stool
Dawn brings out my cardboard box and says
"I knew this was yours"
Then Tony, the owner, appears
Hands me a glass of red wine on the house
And winks

That's why I always say
Let's go Italian!

The Cedar Chest

For many years
Every Friday night we were at the cabin in cool weather
We stopped at The Cedar Chest
For the AYCE fish fry
And maybe a bowl of Ted's corn chowder
It stands just a ways out of town
On a hillside overlooking Pine Lake
The ambiance many years ago was crude
Especially the 100+ bras hanging over the bar area
Red satin, lavender flowered, black lace,
Dirty white Playtex with spiral stitched cups
Nude mesh, blue nylon with foam inserts
That gathered dust and remained grungy

Kathy, the owner, never forgot our faces
She always gestured us with
"Hi, guys. The usual?"

Locals dotted the bar stools
Generous guts spilling over waistbands
As we sucked in the chaos of the pool table
The country music
The consistent chatter

Now the décor has been upgraded
Newer tables, chairs, bar stools, carpeting
The bathrooms have been redone
There is a big screen TV
A faux fireplace
And a huge lakeside deck

We no longer indulge in fried fish
Instead, we nosh on the best burgers found anywhere
Medium-rare with grilled onions
And a side of hand-cut fries
Always cooked perfectly

The bras have disappeared
No longer dangling in the dim light
Adding fodder for conversation
And collecting dust
They are no longer a nod to the restaurant's name
Just a memory
And a testament to the changing times

Norway Nuances

On the shore of Kingsley Lake
Off County Road 39
Is Norway Ridge Supper Club
In its hunter green cedar shake glory
It is solemnly propped on a forested hill
In an organic, earthy, looming kind of innocence
That has served northern Minnesota
Since 1948

It welcomes customers to sample home-smoked ribs
Scratch-made sauces and dressings
And excellent craft cocktails
There is nothing vague about the bartender
When he shakes up a
Bombay gin martini
The liquid shivering in an iced glass
Clenched around a lemon twist
Or blue cheese stuffed olive
Dissolving the citrus and salt to marry the flavors
His radio voice bellowing and resonant

I always begin my experience with a martini
On the rocks
As ice clinks against the glass
My fingers flex to grip the frosty crystals
And I scan the extensive menu
Knowing I will order the walleye or sunfish

Jerry relishes the prime rib
Medium-rare, thick cut, juicy, fatty and succulent

The mound of sunnies wins out
Lightly crunchy and melt-in-the-mouth good
Accompanied by parmesan potato skins
With creamy dipping sauce
Wild rice soup
Thick and studded with carrots, celery, onions
And hunks of chicken
The basket of rolls is intriguing
But I decide no extra carbs
And dive into my entrée with waggled hands
All the while
Tilting my head in awe
Of the rustic interior
With bloated, stuffed wall fish, skis, pinecones
Protruding from every log
Realizing the relaxing ambiance
Is Norway nuance

Wharf Whimsy

When we purchased our Crosslake cabin
Twenty years ago
The Wharf held heaps of nostalgia
It was tinged with memories of our brief honeymoon
Floating before our eyes
As we sipped chilled Happy Hour martinis
On Friday evenings
After a three-hour drive from home

The white painted cabin
Stark and pooled in foot-high grasses
Nondescript, limp in its historic board structure
Smiled back at us
From across the channel
Almost distorted like a shivering statue
A venomous imposter
We had previously commented on the unlikeliness
That it still stood

Winters at the Wharf were the best
The channel current streamed through shaded ice
And we warmed our tummies
With steak sandwiches for $7.95
Shuddering at the silvery snowflakes
Manically finding their places
Either to mound in crystal shivers
Or dissipate in frigid flow
Like a plume of cigar smoke

Our litany of love continued in summer
When we'd dock our pontoon
In whooshing rivulets of no wake waves
Tie up the steely vessel
Sit outside at a white plastic table
Order a beer and a burger
Watch the sputtering boats glide by
Occasionally wave
And relish in the lapping curls
Creating the Up North Wharf Whimsy

Lundrigan's Lost

Twenty years ago
Lundrigan's opened in Crosslake
An upper-end boutique
For men, women, and even kids
With name brands
Like Woolrich, North Face, Nautica, Free People
Even Tommy Bahama
Solid styles
Especially for the more mature clientele
Seasonal colors to allure
Oodles of charm on which to splurge
Not just blotches on rotating racks
But glaciers of festive and classic merging together

Leisurewear was grouped by color or label
With novel beach bags, purses and scarves
Perched atop the racks
As magnetic décor

There was no snail pace here
If you wanted your size
You grabbed and headed to the dressing room
Drenched yourself in frothy forward fashion
Without lingering
Snapped out of a drowsy state
Embellished the outfit with earrings from the glass case

Stirred up your venom and eradicated the gloom
With a cute sun hat
Or Crosslake sweatshirt
Because your fingers were now nimble
And these fashions had just premiered
You guzzled with passion

However
The vibrant vine of excitement
In the Town Square shop
Is no longer

And that is why
I am sad
Lundrigan's is
Now lost
Forever

Celebrate! Celebrate!

Crosslake celebrations
St. Patrick's Day and Crosslake Days
Are annual traditions

In March thousands flock from many miles
To tousle their hair with green
And don layers of beads
Wear green hats, green T-shirts, green face paint
Route 66 is road blocked
Beer stands are stationed along the road
People ponder for hours to watch the parade
Yell until their voices are raspy
With hair falling in curtains
Around their green faces
Smashing beers down their gullets
Freckling the streets with litter

And the last weekend in September
Crosslake Days quash out any mundane activities
Patron groups are thinner than St. Paddy Day
But the celebratory attitude is there
And the thud of activity prevails
My favorite is the Jul Bazaar
At the Lutheran church
Where I arrive before 9 am
And stand outside in line

Swathed in a sweater
I quickly enter when the doors open
Grab my canvas bag
Scan the goods
And head straight for the lefse table
Grab several baggies of the Scandinavian delight
Stop for crocheted potholders
And head for the checkout table

Beginning at noon we savor the chili cook off
Sampling beef and chicken versions
From several businesses
Cast our votes for the best
Then stop by the arts and crafts fair
Where I purchase handmade soap
And beaded bracelets
Which I slip on
To celebrate! Celebrate!
Crosslake style

Loon Love

A pontoon boat ride at the cabin
Is a gift we give ourselves
A nature nurture
After packing a soft-sided cooler
With drinks, ice, cheese and fruit
Stuffing a bag with sunscreen, phones
Lip protector, and credit card
We hop on the golf cart and barrel down the slope
To the dock
To surrender the boat from the lift

We pile on like wizards of water
Waiting for our encore
Ducking to avoid the flapping lift canopy
Unvocal as our chariot backs out
Into the tepid lake
We exhale
A subtle tribute to the oasis awaiting us

The boat is our temple of survival
Acting as castaways from the clatter of life
Snaking through Daggett Lake
And then through the channel
Becoming nearly drowsy
We are rival rascals
Nodding our heads to Jimmy Buffett tunes

Marveling at the spectral beauty
Zooming across Cross Lake
Past The Wharf and our honeymoon cabin
Still the same whitewashed wood

The pontoon scuttles past the greasy stench
Propelling us through another scenic channel
Into Lower Whitefish Lake
And we hang a right
Cruising into Island
Skirting paddle boarders and jet skiers
Who flock to the lake
To harmonize with serenity

But the special journey is
Through the narrow channel
That requires us to lift the prop
So we don't skim the sand bottom
The motor sputtering in throbbing glee

Past beaver dams
Fastened to fallen birch limbs
Past blooming lily pads
Past a mega mansion
Purportedly owned by
The owner of the Kansas City Chiefs
Uninhabited, as usual
A five-foot tall metal chicken statue

A lopsided white, peeling paint
Log Adirondack chair
Strategically placed on an old wooden dock
We twinge at the charm
Squeeze our drink koozies
Take in the muffled calls of loons
Idling around the boat

And we slump
Huddled in cushioned seats
Plunk an anchor into tiny Loon Lake
Lean back and gush
At our finale of sun-streaked
Liquid rainbows

Liquid Rainbows

For 20 years we have owned a cabin
Tucked in a lovely neighborhood
Of friendly, helpful, sometimes eccentric souls
Near a bay on Daggett Lake
It was our weekend getaway before we retired
Our escape from work
And everyday mundane drudgery
We bought a pontoon boat from C&C
Cruised the chain with ardor and a cooler full of beer
The porta potty always filled and ready
We shopped Crosslake, Nisswa, Pequot Lakes
Pine River and Emily
When boutiques were plentiful
And small town dives hummed
We roasted hot dogs at the fire pit with grandkids
Zipped to the lake in a golf cart
Gazed at the constellations in below zero temps
Then retreated to the garage
Where we lit a fire in the old wood stove
Struck matches to light vanilla-scented candles
And basked in their glow
We attended Scandinavian Days, Crosslake Days
St. Paddy's parades, pig roasts, 4th of July fireworks
Wooden boat shows, Bean Hole Days
And October fest
The art shows and book sales
Were dear to my heart

We removed our hummingbird feeder
After the black bear drained and rearranged it
We fished off the dock
Played Scrabble and Yahtzee on winter nights
Took long walks on a winding road
Grilled juicy Lucy's on Memorial weekend
And partied with our neighbors
Late into the night

But my favorite memory
Is mentally drifting away
On the pontoon
In sweet seduction
The splashing lake water
Lifting high into deep blue sky
Like Lucy in the sky with diamonds
To reach
Liquid rainbows

CPSIA information can be obtained
at www.ICGtesting.com
Printed in the USA
FSHW011332290521
81828FS

9 781614 937739